MOMENTS WITH MARY

JOURNEY WITH MARY THROUGH HER MOMENTS OF JOY AND SORROW

FATHER GUS

WELLSPRING PUBLICATIONS

About the Cover

The Pomegranate is one of the symbols for Mary, the mother of Jesus and for the Church as it symbolizes fruitfulness and unity with the Will of God. The seeds are close to one another symbolizing unity. Every part of the tree and every bit of the fruit from the skin to the core has meaning, value and the power to heal.

Art Credit: Shannon Lutmer

CONTENTS

METHOD OF MEDITATION

Spiritual masters have offered many different methods and ways of meditation and contemplation over the years. You may have an approach of your own or have adopted one of the existing methods. I hope the following helps you with your contemplative walk with Mary, our Mother of Compassion

* * *

EXPERIENCE

Be still with the given image or picture for a few moments. Then, prayerfully read the given Scripture passage.

* * *

REFLECTION

Be still for a few moments after reading. Mediate, ponder, reflect, or contemplate the feelings, ideas, images, thoughts, etc. that come to mind at this time.

* * *

CHOICE

Choose the feeling, idea, image, thought or a call to action that stands out for you at this time. Be still with it a little longer and choose a response.

* * *

ACTION

Act on the choice you made. This is your committed response to what the Lord has spoken to you in your meditation.

* * *

JOURNAL

Briefly write in your journal what the Lord said to you or how the Lord moved you in your meditation and how you have responded.

PREPARING FOR MEDITATION

BE STILL AND KNOW THAT I AM GOD.

— PSALM 46:11

Be in your prayer space, follow your usual rituals and settle into silence. If you don't have a ritual of your own, the following may be helpful.

Be in your prayer space. Assume a comfortable posture. Take a few, deep, gentle, and slow breaths and settle into silence and stillness.

Consecrate your time - this moment and all that comes with this moment...in your own way, in humble, simple, maybe even inadequate words, gestures, or rituals.

* * *

Now from the depth of your heart begin to wish your mind well...

(Choose one or more of the blessings below or something similar and keep repeating them in your heart until your mind and heart calm down to serenity and peace and begin your meditation)

Bless the Lord O my soul... Let all that is within me give God praise!
Bless the Lord O my soul...Let me never forget your blessings!
Bless the Lord O my soul...Let me feel your presence!

May my mind be clear, open, and free...
May all negative thoughts drift away like clouds...
May my mind be filled with comfort, ease, peace, serenity ...

May my heart be pure that I may see you...
May my heart be humble that I may hear you...
May my heart be loving that I may serve you...

May my heart be noble that I may reflect you...
May my heart be trusting that I may be safe in you...
May my heart be hopeful that I may be free in you...

May my heart be faithful that I may do your will...
May my heart be open that I may hear your word...
May my heart be serene that I may abide in you...

* * *

Journal – at the end of your meditation...

Use the last few minutes to write down whatever is on your mind at this moment - your insights, thoughts, feelings, etc. and your choice of action

PREFACE

We are blessed with many Marian prayers, hymns, songs, and devotional practices. The following is not meant to be another Marian devotion. It is meant to be a contemplative walk with Mary through the many joyful and sorrowful moments in her life. Pope Francis said that having a devotion to the Blessed

Virgin Mary isn't just something that is nice or good to do but is an obligation in the life of a Christian (January 1, 2018). Mary is a gentle woman, a faithful woman, a loving woman, a self-sacrificing woman and above all a compassionate mother.

Mary, as the Mother of Compassion, has always been a fearless, powerful, moving, gentle, joyful, and strong figure in the history of the spiritual tradition of the Church. She joyfully said "yes" to the word of the angel from God; she brought joy to her cousin, Elizabeth, and shared her joy as well; she brought joy to a wedding party that ran out of wine; she rejoiced at the finding of her son in the temple; she rejoiced with the apostles in the upper room after the resurrection of Jesus. She was a woman of joy!

She stood fearlessly at the cross while others fled. She stood strong seeing her son beaten, bruised, and placed under the burden of the cross. She was courageous and unafraid to stand by the cross as her son hung on the cross and welcomed her son's lifeless body into her arms. She stepped into the pain, rejection, loneliness, anguish, and passion of her son, and also that of his disciples, without going under. She stood strong and steadfast for her son and his disciples. She became strength for the suffering, lonely, rejected and the sorrowful. She emerged from her pain and sorrow to become for us a fearless, powerful, courageous, and moving figure. She was also a woman of sorrow.

Mary is a woman of compassion – sharing in the joy and pain of humanity. Compassion is a sharing in the passion of others - the joy and the sorrow of others.

The following is an invitation to make a contemplative walk with Mary through the many joyful and sorrowful moments in her life. I hope that this journey with Mary will bless you and enable you to make your own journey faithfully and joyfully as she did. It is my hope and prayer that the Mother of Compassion will inspire you to have confidence, stand strong during difficult moments, rejoice during joy-filled moments, be grateful during grace-filled moments and to have peace. May the Mother of Compassion be a source of blessing, grace, and strength for us all.

The Angel Announces the Birth of Jesus

Be still for a few moments!

In the sixth month, the angel Gabriel was sent from God to a town of Galilee called Nazareth, to a virgin betrothed to a man named Joseph, of the house of David, and the virgin's name was Mary. And coming to her, he said, "Hail, favored one! The Lord is with you." But she was greatly troubled at what was said and pondered what sort of greeting this might be. Then the angel said to her, "Do not be afraid, Mary, for you have found favor with God. Behold, you will conceive in your womb and bear a son, and you shall name him Jesus. He will be great and will be called Son of the Most High, and the Lord God will give him the throne of David his father, and he will rule over the house of Jacob forever, and of his kingdom there will be no end." But Mary said to the angel, "How can this be, since I have no relations with a man?" And the angel said to her in reply, "The holy Spirit will come upon you, and the power of the Most High will overshadow you. Therefore, the child to be born will be called holy, the Son of God. And behold, Elizabeth, your relative, has also conceived a son in her old age, and this is the sixth month for her who was called barren; for nothing will be impossible for God." Mary said, "Behold, I am the handmaid of the Lord. May it be done to me according to your word." Then the angel departed from her. (Luke 1:26-38)

* * *

Be still for a few moments!

* * *

Prayerfully reflect...

The angel said, "Do not be afraid, Mary, for you have found favor with God."

Be Still! Meditate on finding favor with God!

Nothing will be impossible with God!

Reflect on renewing your confidence in God's provident care!

Mary said, "I am the handmaid of the Lord. May it be done to me according to your word!"

Reflect on surrendering to God's plan and purpose for you!

Mary trusted and surrendered to God's word and God's word became flesh in her. God's word comes to us today through the Scriptures, through lived experiences of many people, through our own personal experiences and through many events and situations. We are called to be sensitive, docile, available, and attentive to God's word and let God's word become flesh in our life.

* * *

Be still and listen for a few moments!

Pray for God's wisdom to know His plan and for the courage to fulfill His plan for you.

Pray for the grace to let God's word become flesh in your own life today!

Mary Visits Her Cousin, Elizabeth

Be still for a few moments!

During those days Mary set out and traveled to the hill country in haste to a town of Judah, where she entered the house of Zechariah and greeted Elizabeth. When Elizabeth heard Mary's greeting, the infant leaped in her womb, and Elizabeth, filled with the holy Spirit, cried out in a loud voice and said, "Most blessed are you among women, and blessed is the fruit of your womb. And how does this happen to me, that the mother of my Lord should come to me? For at the moment the sound of your greeting reached my ears, the infant in my womb leaped for joy. Blessed are you who believed that what was spoken to you by the Lord would be fulfilled."

And Mary said: "My soul proclaims the greatness of the Lord; my spirit rejoices in God my savior. For he has looked upon his handmaid's lowliness; behold, from now on will all ages call me blessed. The Mighty One has done great things for me, and holy is his name. His mercy is from age to age to those who fear him. He has shown might with his arm, dispersed the arrogant of mind and heart. He has thrown down the rulers from their thrones but lifted up the lowly. The hungry he has filled with good things; the rich he has sent away empty. He has helped Israel his servant, remembering his mercy, according to his promise to our fathers, to Abraham and to his descendants forever." Mary remained with her about three months and then returned to her home. (Luke 1:39-56)

* * *

Be still for a few moments!

* * *

Prayerfully reflect...

Mary visited her cousin, Elizabeth, and gave her much joy, comfort and courage. They truly became a source of blessing and Grace for each other as they shared how God was working through them and through the new lives that they were nurturing within them.

Reflect on bringing joy to others and being a blessing to others!

Mary reached out to her cousin in need while she herself was in great need and had her own personal concerns.

Reflect on reaching out to others, even beyond your own personal concerns and needs.

Mary stirred up life in Elizabeth. "The moment your greeting sounded in my ears, the baby stirred in my womb for joy," said Elizabeth.

Reflect on stirring up life in others.

* * *

Be still and listen for a few moments!

Mary Gives Birth to Jesus and Lays Him in a Manger

Be still for a few moments!

TRUST
PEACE

In those days a decree went out from Caesar Augustus that the whole world should be enrolled. This was the first enrollment, when Quirinius was governor of Syria. So all went to be enrolled, each to his own town. And Joseph too went up from Galilee from the town of Nazareth to Judea, to the city of David that is called Bethlehem, because he was of the house and family of David, to be enrolled with Mary, his betrothed, who was with child. While they were there, the time came for her to have her child, and she gave birth to her firstborn son. She wrapped him in swaddling clothes and laid him in a manger, because there was no room for them in the inn. (Luke 2:1-7)

* * *

Be still for a few moments!

* * *

Prayerfully reflect......

The creator of the universe is born of a young Galilean girl, wrapped in swaddling clothes, and laid in a manger because there was no room in the inn! How amazing!

Reflect on this incredible revelation of "all-embracing love" of God revealed in Jesus!

What does it say to you? How does it inspire you, or challenge you?

Joseph and Mary surrendered to God's plan and were put to great testing times as they learned to surrender. Surrender is a difficult and demanding word! The Gospel demands a response of obedience and self-surrender.

What are your reflections on this call to obedience, to surrender?

The birth of a baby is always an act of trust, much more so the birth of the divine baby. Any baby born into the world is an act of trust in the future of humanity. The birth of Jesus called forth even greater trust than could be imagined. The circumstances of his birth were extraordinary and even mysterious. Mary had to trust; Joseph had to trust; Elizabeth had to trust; Zechariah had to trust - And God himself trusted... trusting a young Galilean girl with a baby to be the Messiah is an amazing story of "TRUST"!

What are your reflections on this call to trust?

* * *

Be still and listen for a few moments!

Mary, Joseph, & Jesus Flee into Egypt

Be still for a few moments!

When they had departed, behold, the angel of the Lord appeared to Joseph in a dream and said, "Rise, take the child and his mother, flee to Egypt, and stay there until I tell you. Herod is going to search for the child to destroy him." Joseph rose and took the child and his mother by night and departed for Egypt. He stayed there until the death of Herod, that what the Lord had said through the prophet might be fulfilled, "Out of Egypt I called my son." (Matthew 2:13-15)

* * *

Be still for a few moments!

* * *

Prayerfully reflect...

This was one of the sad and difficult situation in Mary's life. She had to simply rely on the dream of her spouse, Joseph, and trust his plan as the plan of God for her and her newborn baby. She trusted the man whom God had given to her for her and her child's protection.

Reflect on Mary's unconditional trust! Reflect on the quality of your trust in God's plan!

Do you have a person in your life that you can rely on with the kind of confidence Mary had?

Can you be such a trustworthy person for your family and friends?

Joseph was a safe person to be with. He was "tzaddik," a "just man"- a man of honor, noble, courageous, virtuous, and tenacious.

Be still with this "tzaddik" for a few moments!

Learn from him what it means to be a "tzaddik" – just, noble, virtuous, courageous, and faithful!

Joseph listened and obeyed the voice of God. He was willing to invest all he had to keep the baby and mother safe from all dangers. He was willing to move from place to place until he could settle into a situation where the mother and child would be safe.

Reflect on imitating Joseph in listening to God and obeying his word!

Be a safe person to be with and be concerned about the safety of others as Joseph was!

Create and cultivate a safe environment for all.

MARY AND JOSEPH PRESENT JESUS IN THE TEMPLE

Be still for a few moments!

When the days were completed for their purification according to the law of Moses, they took him up to Jerusalem to present him to the Lord, just as it is written in the law of the Lord, "Every male that opens the womb shall be consecrated to the Lord," and to offer the sacrifice of "a pair of turtledoves or two young pigeons," in accordance with the dictate in the law of the Lord. Now there was a man in Jerusalem whose name was Simeon. This man was righteous and devout, awaiting the consolation of Israel, and the holy Spirit was upon him. It had been revealed to him by the holy Spirit that he should not see death before he had seen the Messiah of the Lord. He came in the Spirit into the temple; and when the parents brought in the child Jesus to perform the custom of the law in regard to him, he took him into his arms and blessed God, saying: "Now, Master, you may let your servant go in peace, according to your word, for my eyes have seen your salvation, which you prepared in sight of all the peoples, a light for revelation to the Gentiles, and glory for your people Israel." The child's father and mother were amazed at what was said about him; and Simeon blessed them and said to Mary his mother, "Behold, this child is destined for the fall and rise of many in Israel, and to be a sign that will be contradicted (and you yourself a sword will pierce) so that the thoughts of many hearts may be revealed." (Luke 2:22-33)

* * *

Be still for a few moments!

* * *

Prayerfully reflect......

Mary and Joseph consecrated Jesus in obedience to the Law of Moses.

Be still for a moment and meditate on the fidelity of Mary and Joseph!
Reflect on the quality of your own faithfulness to the law of God!

Seeing Mary and Joseph and their baby, Simeon, a holy and wise old man, rejoiced and sang his song of surrender. Simeon saw all that he hoped to see and he was ready to return to his master. Simeon was a man of hope, and his hope was fulfilled in his vision of Jesus.

Reflect on being men and women of hope!
Let your hope be fulfilled in Jesus!

Simeon sang a song of surrender.

Sing your own song of self-surrender.

Pray for the wisdom to know God's plan and the courage to surrender to his plan for you.

Simeon Prophesizes about Jesus and Mary

Be still for a few moments!

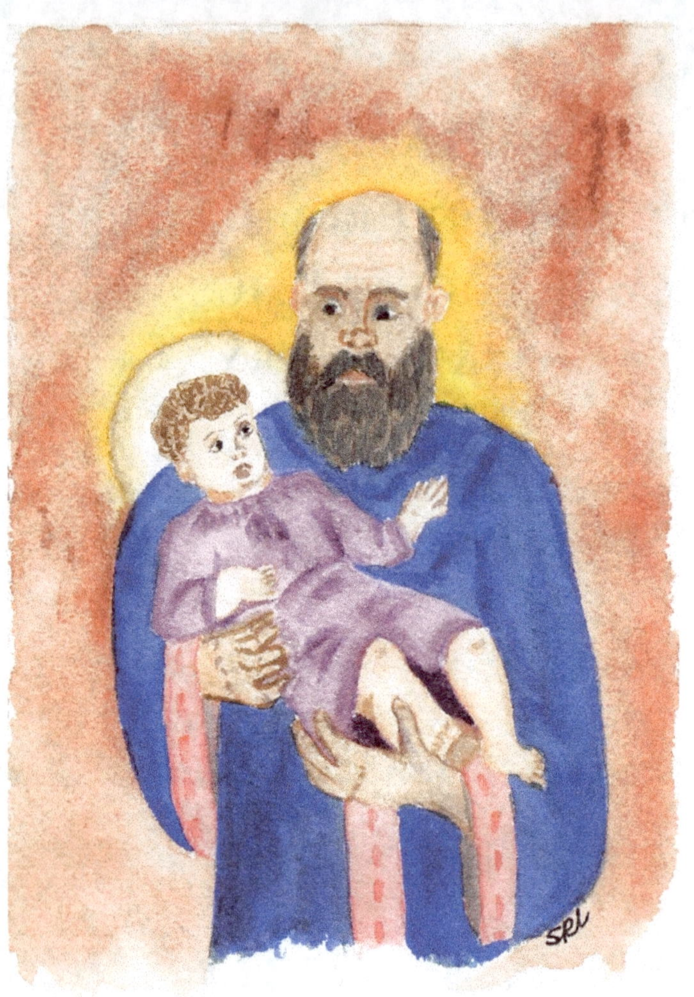

The child's father and mother were amazed at what was said about him; and Simeon blessed them and said to Mary his mother, "Behold, this child is destined for the fall and rise of many in Israel, and to be a sign that will be contradicted (and you yourself a sword will pierce) so that the thoughts of many hearts may be revealed." (Luke 2:33-35)

* * *

Be still for a few moments!

* * *

Prayerfully reflect......

When Mary and Joseph brought Jesus to the temple in Jerusalem, Simeon took Jesus in his arms and sang a beautiful prayer song. He sang of his readiness to die in peace now that he had seen the messiah. This vision of the messiah was enough...life was fulfilled.... hunger and thirst were satisfied.

Listen to what Jesus says, "Blessed are they who hunger and thirst for holiness: they shall have their fill." (Matthew 5:6)

St. Augustine said: "Our hearts are restless until they rest in God." This is what Jeremiah had to say: "When you look (search) for me, you will find me. Yes, when you seek me with all your heart...you will find me.... I will let you find me...." (Jeremiah 29:13ff). Simeon saw the one he was longing for!

Be still for a few moments!
Get in touch with your own inner longings!
Become aware of your own desires, the desires of your hearts!
Bless yourself with good, noble, wholesome, and redeeming desires!

Simeon also spoke of sadness that would come and pierce the heart of Mary.

Remember the many mothers whose hearts are pierced because of the sufferings of their children.

Simeon called Jesus "a light to the nations." Jesus called us to "be the light of the world."

Reflect on this call...on the blessing and grace of being in the light of Jesus and on the responsibility that comes with being called to be light to the world.

Mary and Joseph Miss Jesus on their Journey Home

Be still for a few moments!

Each year his parents went to Jerusalem for the feast of Passover and when he was twelve years old, they went up according to festival custom. After they had completed its days, as they were returning, the boy Jesus remained behind in Jerusalem, but his parents did not know it. Thinking that he was in the caravan, they journeyed for a day and looked for him among their relatives and acquaintances, but not finding him, they returned to Jerusalem to look for him. (Luke 2:41-45)

* * *

Be still for a few moments!

* * *

Prayerfully reflect...

The law required every adult male Jew who lived within fifteen miles of Jerusalem to attend the Passover. In fact, it was the aim of every Jew to attend the feast at least once in his lifetime.

Be still for a few moments!

Reflect on the longing of a Jew to attend the feast of the Passover and your own longing to attend "The Passover," "The Eucharist," available to us every day where we are and not have to go to Jerusalem.

A Jewish boy became a man when he was twelve. Then he became a son of the law and had to take the obligation of the law upon him. So, at the age of twelve, Jesus went to the Passover for the first time.

Reflect on the longing of a young man to go for such an awesome experience!

Can you think of a time when you longed for something that you never had before

or something that you believed would be a great and awesome experience?

After they had completed its days, as they were returning, the boy Jesus remained behind in Jerusalem, but his parents did not know it.

Reflect on the feelings of Mary and Joseph who lost their only son!

Remember fathers and mothers who grieve the loss of their children and pray with them.

Remember mothers and fathers who have lost their babies before they had a chance to see the world.

Walk with those who grieve the loss of parents or children or any other kind of losses.

Mary and Joseph Find Jesus in the Temple

Be still for a few moments!

After three days they found him in the temple, sitting in the midst of the teachers, listening to them and asking them questions, and all who heard him were astounded at his understanding and his answers. When his parents saw him, they were astonished, and his mother said to him, "Son, why have you done this to us? Your father and I have been looking for you with great anxiety." And he said to them, "Why were you looking for me? Did you not know that I must be in my Father's house?" But they did not understand what he said to them. He went down with them and came to Nazareth and was obedient to them; and his mother kept all these things in her heart. And Jesus advanced [in] wisdom and age and favor before God and man. (Luke 2:46-52)

* * *

Be still for a few moments!

* * *

Prayerfully reflect...

Joseph and Mary anxiously searched for their lost son for three days, found him in the temple, took him to the safety of their home where he grew in wisdom, knowledge and age. It is in the safety of an ordinary home, in a safe and loving environment that children can grow up to be mature, free, joyful, faith-filled, virtuous, and wise men and women.

Reflect on nurturing a safe environment for all, especially children and the vulnerable!

Reflect on making your home a safe place, a sanctuary for yourself, for your spouse, for your children, for your parents, for your neighbors.

Be safe! Look out for safety of others!

Reflect on being grateful - grateful for your family, however imperfect or broken it may be!

Be grateful for your spouse, for your children, for your parents however, imperfect they may be!

Mary and Jesus Attend the Wedding in Cana

Be still for a few moments!

On the third day there was a wedding in Cana in Galilee, and the mother of Jesus was there. Jesus and his disciples were also invited to the wedding. When the wine ran short, the mother of Jesus said to him, "They have no wine." [And] Jesus said to her, "Woman, how does your concern affect me? My hour has not yet come." His mother said to the servers, "Do whatever he tells you." Now there were six stone water jars there for Jewish ceremonial washings, each holding twenty to thirty gallons. Jesus told them, "Fill the jars with water." So, they filled them to the brim. Then he told them, "Draw some out now and take it to the headwaiter." So, they took it. And when the headwaiter tasted the water that had become wine, without knowing where it came from (although the servers who had drawn the water knew), the headwaiter called the bridegroom and said to him, "Everyone serves good wine first, and then when people have drunk freely, an inferior one; but you have kept the good wine until now." (John 2: 1-10)

* * *

Be still for a few moments!

* * *

Prayerfully reflect......

The hosts ran out of wine at the wedding in Cana. Mary said to Jesus, "They have no wine." How attentive and sensitive Mary was. She stepped into an embarrassing moment!

Reflect on being attentive and sensitive to the concerns and needs of others, especially those embarrassing situations.

Jesus said, "My time has not yet come."

Reflect on waiting patiently, waiting for the right time, God's time!

Jesus changed water into wine and thus provided an abundance of fine quality wine!

Reflect on the transforming power of Jesus.

It was the water used for ceremonial purification that Jesus turned into choice wine. Jesus had come to replace the religious customs and institutions of Israel with himself. No longer would washing with water be a means of achieving purity or holiness. Purification or holiness would be achieved by accepting the new wine Jesus offered. This new wine of his wisdom is more precious and a profoundly more effective means of salvation than anything that had preceded it, including the Jewish law which was often described by the rabbis as a font of living water.

Be still for a few moments!
Meditate on the purifying, life-changing and life-transforming power of Jesus.

Mary Visits Jesus During His Ministry

Be still for a few moments!

YES
May it be done to me according to your word.

While he was still speaking to the crowds, his mother and his brothers appeared outside, wishing to speak with him. Someone told him, "Your mother and your brothers are standing outside, asking to speak with you." But he said in reply to the one who told him, "Who is my mother? Who are my brothers?" And stretching out his hand toward his disciples, he said, "Here are my mother and my brothers. For whoever does the will of my heavenly Father is my brother, and sister, and mother." (Mathew 12:46-50)

* * *

Be still for a few moments!

* * *

Prayerfully reflect......

Jesus said, "Who is my mother and who are my brothers... whoever does the will of my Father is brother and sister and mother to me." Jesus spoke of a new kind of relationship...one that goes far beyond blood relationships. Nothing can break the "blood connection" and yet we know that "blood ties" don't necessarily create a bond of love, dedication or affection.

Real relationships, true connections and bonds of love are established around shared goals, shared ideals, shared causes, shared obedience, shared fidelity, and shared hopes.

Reflect on developing relationships beyond family and friendship circles and forming community with others who share your faith.

Jesus calls us to enter into a relationship of love and obedience...an obedience that binds us together as brothers and sisters of Jesus, sons and daughters of the Heavenly Father.

Our common obedience makes us true brothers and sisters.

Dwell on this for some time.

MARY MEETS JESUS CARRYING THE CROSS

BE STILL FOR A FEW MOMENTS!

A large crowd of people followed Jesus, including many women who mourned and lamented him. Jesus turned to them and said, "Daughters of Jerusalem, do not weep for me; weep instead for yourselves and for your children, for indeed, the days are coming when people will say, 'Blessed are the barren, the wombs that never bore and the breasts that never nursed.' At that time, people will say to the mountains, 'Fall upon us!' and to the hills, 'Cover us!' for if these things are done when the wood is green what will happen when it is dry?" (Luke 23:28-31)

* * *

Be still for a few moments!

* * *

Prayerfully reflect...

Jesus looked beyond his pain to attend to the pain of the women who were following him on his way to Calvary.

**Reflect on looking beyond yourself, beyond your concerns, needs and pains
and attending to those of others.**

The Gospel speaks of women following Jesus on his way to Calvary. Mary's name is not mentioned. However, it is certain that she would have been among the women who followed Jesus – it is unlikely that she wasn't there.

Think about many women who suffer and are burdened because of the choices their children make. Some women suffer because of the disappointments, sufferings or pains of their children who make courageous choices and strive to lead a decent and virtuous life. Other women suffer because of the poor choices their children make.

Bless the mothers who suffer and walk with them in prayer.

Support the women who must carry heavy burdens.

Mary Stands at the Foot of the Cross

Be still for a few moments!

Standing by the cross of Jesus were his mother and his mother's sister, Mary the wife of Clopas, and Mary of Magdala. When Jesus saw his mother and the disciple there whom he loved, he said to his mother, "Woman, behold, your son." Then he said to the disciple, "Behold, your mother." And from that hour the disciple took her into his home. (John 19:25-27)

* * *

Be still for a few moments!

* * *

Three women are mentioned standing by the cross. Mary, the mother of Jesus, was among them.

Imagine, if you can, standing by the cross of someone you love!

Think of the many women who have to stand by the sufferings of their children.

Perhaps, you know someone who is standing by the cross of their children. Be with them in prayer.

Jesus saw his mother and the disciple whom he loved beyond his own pains and sufferings during his dying moments.

Reflect on looking beyond your own pains and sufferings and becoming sensitive to the suffering of others around you and beyond your family and friendship circles.

Hold them in your heart in prayer.

Mother and disciple came into mutual care and concern. Mary became mother for all disciples.

Let us learn from Mary and be inspired by her compassion, her humility, and her readiness to do what God called her to do.

Her "yes" to the word of the angel from God, was a life-long "yes."

Reflect on saying "yes" to the Lord!

Mary Receives the Body of Jesus

Be still for a few moments!

Now there was a virtuous and righteous man named Joseph who, though he was a member of the council, had not consented to their plan of action. He came from the Jewish town of Arimathea and was awaiting the kingdom of God. He went to Pilate and asked for the body of Jesus. After he had taken the body down, he wrapped it in a linen cloth and laid him in a rock-hewn tomb in which no one had yet been buried. (Luke 23:50-53)

* * *

Be still for a few moments!

* * *

Prayerfully reflect...

Joseph of Arimathea took the body of Jesus down from the cross with the approval of Pilate. The Gospel does not give us many more details, nor does it say that the body was placed in the arms of his mother. However, tradition tells us that the body of Jesus was placed in the arms of his mother. Images of Mary holding the body of her son have been honored throughout history.

Mary, the mother of Jesus, stood fearlessly at the cross while others fled. She stood strong seeing her son beaten, bruised, and placed under the burden of the cross. She was courageous and unafraid to stand by the cross as her son hung on the cross. She definitely would have been unafraid to welcome her son's lifeless body into her arms.

Meditate on the courage and compassion of Mary. Pray for courage and compassion!

Mary was a true woman and a mother of compassion, who, as a young woman, sang the song of mercy, "His mercy is from age to age to those who fear him" (Luke 1:50). She is the icon, the image of the mother of mercy. Mary is the mother of compassion. She is definitely an image of hope, courage, strength, and wisdom.

May the Mother of Compassion be a source of Grace and strength for us all.

Think of mothers who have to receive lifeless bodies of their children in many forms and be with them in prayer. Bless and pray with those mothers who must receive lifeless bodies of their stillborn children.

Mary Witnesses the Burial of Jesus

Be still for a few moments!

When it was evening, there came a rich man from Arimathea named Joseph, who was himself a disciple of Jesus. He went to Pilate and asked for the body of Jesus; then Pilate ordered it to be handed over. Taking the body, Joseph wrapped it [in] clean linen and laid it in his new tomb that he had hewn in the rock. Then he rolled a huge stone across the entrance to the tomb and departed. (Matthew 27:57-60)

* * *

Be still for a few moments!

* * *

Prayerfully reflect...

Jesus was born in a borrowed stable and then he was buried in a borrowed tomb. He said to one of those who wanted to follow him, "Foxes have holes and the birds of the air have nests, but the Son of man has nowhere to lay his head" (Matthew 8:20). Jesus was free, tied down to no place on earth.

Reflect on what that means for you today.

The body of Jesus was prepared for burial. Joseph of Arimathea gave his own tomb to Jesus and laid the body of Jesus there and rolled a large stone in front of it and went home.

What does this mean for you today, two thousand years later?

Reflect on Joseph of Arimathea risking his own life as he accepted Jesus' body for burial.

Reflect on Joseph giving his own tomb and what it calls forth from you today.

**The Lord of the earth goes down into the earth.
Earth has been blessed all over again in a more profound way.**

Meditate on this thought for a few moments.

Mary is with the Disciples in the Upper Room

Be still for a few moments!

While they were looking intently at the sky as he was going, suddenly two men dressed in white garments stood beside them. They said, "Men of Galilee, why are you standing there looking at the sky? This Jesus who has been taken up from you into heaven will return in the same way as you have seen him going into heaven." Then they returned to Jerusalem from the mount called Olivet, which is near Jerusalem, a sabbath day's journey away. When they entered the city, they went to the upper room where they were staying, Peter and John and James and Andrew, Philip and Thomas, Bartholomew and Matthew, James son of Alphaeus, Simon the Zealot, and Judas son of James. All these devoted themselves with one accord to prayer, together with some women, and Mary the mother of Jesus, and his brothers. (Acts 1:10-14)

* * *

Be still for a few moments!

* * *

Prayerfully reflect...

This is a moment of sorrow and joy at the same time. Sorrow had come to the disciples because their master was gone. Joy had come because of the assurance that he would return. With joy and sorrow, they went to the upper room and prayed. Sorrow and joy brought them together with Mary, the mother of Jesus, and the other unnamed women. They were together. They prayed. They waited.

Be still with Mary and the disciples for a few moments! Remember those who are grieving the loss of loved ones.

Reflect on the feelings of those whose loved ones have gone away from them and don't know when they will meet again.

Many have gone to distant lands searching for jobs, searching for the meaning of life, and wandering in the wilderness looking for the pleasures of life.

Think of the feelings of those parents, brothers, sisters, and friends who wait and long for their return.

Pray with them.

The disciples waited patiently and prayerfully for the Holy Spirit to come.

Reflect on waiting for the Holy Spirit's guidance for you now.

Closing Prayer and Meditation

Be still for a few moments!

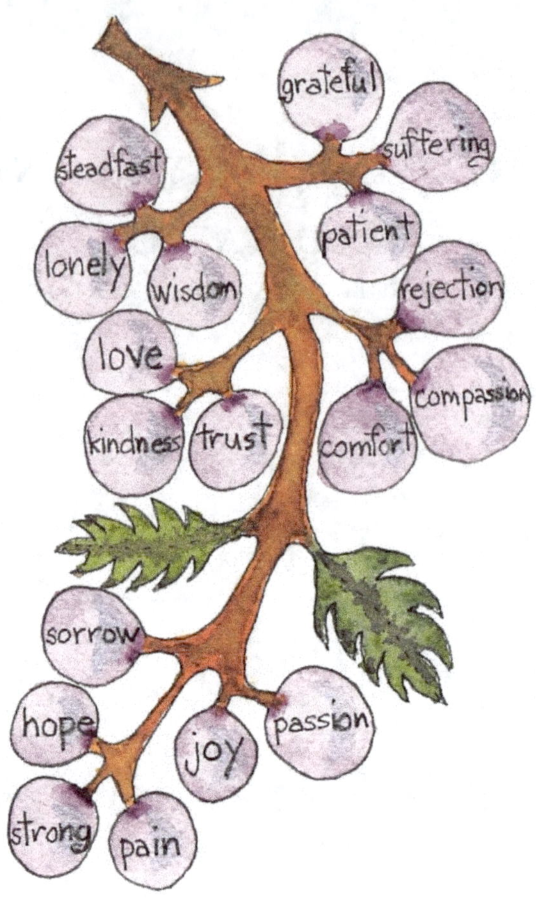

grateful
suffering
steadfast
patient
lonely
wisdom
rejection
love
compassion
kindness
trust
comfort
sorrow
hope
joy
passion
strong
pain

We have just made a journey with Mary and contemplated her moments of joy and sorrow. Rejoicing and celebrating, mourning and grieving are parts of the human condition. No one who cares for others can live long without experiencing joy and sorrow. The Arabs have a proverb: "All sunshine makes a desert." There are certain things only the rain can produce and certain experiences only sorrow can bring. Sorrow can reveal the kindness, comfort and compassion of God and of other human persons. Native Americans describe spirituality as a "moist heart." The native wisdom knew that the soil of the human heart is watered with tears and that tears keep the ground soft and from such ground new life is born. I invite you to take a few moments to reflect on those times when your heart was moist and what emerged from your moist heart.

A challenge for believers is to be signs that inspire hope in moments of joy as well as sorrow. Mary is such a sign of hope for the world. She rejoiced with the good news she heard and brought joy to others. She stepped into the pain, rejection, and passion of her son and also that of his disciples, without going under. She stood strong and steadfast for her son and for his disciples. She became strength for the suffering, lonely, rejected and the sorrowful.

The many joyful fathers, mothers, brothers, and sisters that I have known over the years teach me to be grateful, to share joy, and be a channel and a sign of joy for others. The many sorrowful fathers, mothers, brothers and sisters that I have known over the years have taught me to trust in divine providence, to wait patiently with open arms, to hope when things seem to fall apart and to believe that with God all things are possible. They continue to teach me that it is possible for us to rise above our sorrowful moments, however deep they may be, and stand strong and tall and be steadfast in God's Grace.

Mary, the Mother of Compassion, is an image of Hope, Courage, Strength, and Wisdom. May the Mother of Compassion be a source of Grace and strength for us all.

-Father Gus

About the Author

Father Gus is a Missionary of Saint Francis de Sales from the state of Kerala, India. As a missionary priest for fifty-two years, he has worked in parishes and missions, taught in high schools, worked as professor and spiritual director in Seminaries, directed retreats for clergy, religious and the laity and founded and directed centers for counseling and spiritual direction and retreats in India and USA. He holds a master's degrees in Theology and Psychology and had training in CPE. He has had a wide range of experience in pastoral ministry, directing retreats, and giving counseling and spiritual direction. Currently, he is the Founder-Director of "Wellspring," Fransalian Center for Spirituality in Tyler, Texas, USA.

www.ingramcontent.com/pod-product-compliance
Lightning Source LLC
Chambersburg PA
CBHW072111150726
47999CB00005B/2002